THE LONELY IN MY VEINS

The Lonely In My Veins

POSTCARDS FROM NOWHERE BY DEAD SOCIETY POET

JR Hataway

JR Hataway

Contents

Copyright © 2023 by JR Hataway

First Printing, 2023

Cover Photo: Mimadeo

As always for Rae,
the girl with sunrise in her eyes

Postcards from Nowhere

Rain this morning
beats down my words
a false death
washed off like watercolor
as thunder whispers its grave truth
I'm writing of love
in frozen syllables
on postcards from nowhere
lost in my own wilderness
trying to describe
the taste of the ocean

Photo: Mykhailo Kopyt

Dust of Wounded Hope

Wide awake at last call
we danced in small town sins
a bulldozer Spring
broke lake ice
with a shotgun blast
our poetry of leftover footprints
in midwestern sand
lost golden hours swept away
eaten by a nondescript acid
oh how we tried
to tie time down
in the dust of wounded hope

The Dead Are Still Walking Around

Cardboard souls crumble
as a pious rain
serenades a dry existence
mortal voices fall on deaf ears
we cannot be trusted,
or so the old folks say
snake oil flows like wine
and the dead are still walking around
they just have new names

Imaginary Friends

Winter holds me
in lonely perfection
of the poet's song
a lyrical rain of old phrases
where damp words
and the tears of my eyes
freeze in the air
blood on my hands
where roses tore to the bone
so rage me in this hostile climate
with fire and rusted blades
I'll keep plundering gems of wisdom
from my imaginary friends

Ghost Writer

I hang my hopes in the stars
as shadows turn
at nature's dark door
bones are weary to the
powerful persuasion
of steadfast blues
I drink to the night
its verses unwritten
just ignore the sounds
from my mouth
my ghost writer
becomes giddy
in moonlight

Rebellion in my Veins

Hope is no remedy
for this lonely season
wrecked in the silence
of its sweet obscenities
choked into submission
as dreams smother
in a field of lost things
grumbling time rips me in two
and I've nothing to be
but jealous of the other me
last seen dancing along
the moon's blade
with rebellion in my veins

Photo: Rithika Gopalakrishnan

Fostering the Ache

The world I walk
feels not my own
son of the wind
that rips the sea
borne of midnight
and atomic moon
walking in wishes
to cheat the devil
at his own game
timid arrows rain
in the hunt to forget
fostering the ache
buried behind the veil
of poetry's song

News of the Day

Minutes fall like rain
as time cracks its whip
on life's dry current
I drink and swear
at the news of the day
headlines hold no humanity
I hide in the words
learned from those before
my dreams anchored
in watercolor visions
of an underwater moon
where we all howl
until we drown

Along a Knife's Edge

In circles of light we danced
siphoning sparks from stars
music of the moon on your skin
undulating in freckled measures
colliding colors in a poetry of scars
love's whisper of tomorrow
along a knife's edge
but for now my pen weeps
burying our nights on the page

Selfish Equation

Joyous pain
falls from my pen
a lament of words
akin to walking on fire
foreign gods
grant another morning
for day to light my bones
and these broken wings
punished by winds
I should have mastered
a selfish equation
but here I remain
bound to chase storms
in a sky so infinite

Answering to No One

A symphony in mist of fire
nocturne of my muse in tune
echoing in a heart so dire
longing caressed by the moon

I hear your name on winds that roam
so hopeless I come undone
free in my fall, a leaf gliding home
and answering to no one

Photo: Oliver Hihn

My Dead House

In gritty calm
and deafening silence
love turned gray in
battles between sun and moon
words of strangers
filled the halls of my emptiness
echoes painting my dead house
I foster my art
in the fluid murmur
of ghosts that no longer
hold the keys

Splinters of My World

The night silently
beats at my window
a hollow of stars
embraces the moon
whitening the trees
and the cool face
of the meadow
where we learned love
nocturnal musings
become confessions
in tired phrases as
loneliness warms its bones
in the fires built from
splinters of my world

Dilemma

The wind is playing in the pines
the windows and door
are open on this mild January night
the water pipe under the house
is still broken from the last freeze
I need to wash my hands…
you see my dilemma

Forget to Remember

I seem to heal in darkness
only to be broken by dawn
at night she dances on the edge of silence
bleeding colors from a magical crown
swimming in air that howls with rage
behind my back
minutes of the day drop like anvils
as I bury the ache in white language of the ocean
so far down I forget to remember

Obscure Reality

Love pours from a heart in glass
the trapdoor nailed shut
in my obscure reality
tentacled ghosts weave
a maze of secrets
buried in poetry's pretty words
a library of chains
where I wipe my mind on the page
a lyrical Rorschach left behind
for you to see what you will

Hat of Fire

The nightlong dance was ours
the hollow filled
with the song of her name
a tantrum on my tongue
now in morning she greets me
in strange innocence of the nameless
her poetry a silken tide of shy dreams
and wearing the sun like a hat of fire

The Last Drop of Rain

The wind is listening
so let's take the long way home
a dance along the edge
with no fear of losing the earth
I'll carve our names
in the rusted chains
that bind innocent bones
to the most secret sins
turn off the news
and let love burn
to the sound of glass
until the last drop of rain

Photo: Fran Jacquier

Poet's Song

Oh what a fool who dares the sea
its derisive tide of razored tongues
drilling the soul's marrow
children of absent gods
dress in sorrow and shame
their painted shouts ignored by the poet
his song a beautiful wreckage
echoed onto paper
swinging for the stars
by the rose's fragile stem

Ticker-tape

Might as well
blame the night
its bastard storm
a collision of time
and bourbon blues
as my head spins
with smoke of
snuffed-out candles
lonely blossoms
in the shadows
of your goodbye
written in blurred headlights
on the window pane
and shredded poetry
becomes ticker-tape

My Garden of Wasted Words

I heard yesterday talking
through bitten nails
under a bird's shadow
passing my hat around
in a beggar's waltz
as razored rainbows
split the tongues of heaven
oh to kick off
these boots of pain
and sing like the waves
as they swallow my toes
a sound never heard
amid the buried anger
in my garden
of wasted words

Ghosts of Winter

Insomniac moon
twist your blade of frozen fire
and pry this night wide open
your cold stare
holds my bones
in joint custody
with the ill wind
blowing right through me
left to consort
with the ghosts of winter
we laugh hysterically
as I tie my own dreams in knots

Dumb Traveler

Endless sky and your potion of stars
labyrinthine muse to a dumb traveler
I turn in circles shaking glass eyes like dice
with no escape in this dance of frozen time
left to crumble and fall,
my song dressed in societal chains
a poetic burning in perjury of a naked soul

Empty Bottles of Your Name

I cannot escape
these reflections of me
the broken ones
upon the lonesome waters
in which I drown
a chaos decorated
with empty bottles of your name
strewn across the meadow
where we danced
where your eyes held me
in their emerald embrace
and love bloomed
on my tongue
but tonight
I'll cinch my heart
in barbed wire
and pray the moon
can still walk me home

Still We Sing Hungry

I carve myself into stories
eyes with shades half drawn
squint at the truth
with fingers to mouth
you watch my inner child
fly a kite with no string
it's not enough
to simply be born
to dance in casualty of hope
like wild dogs
we get used to the rain
but still we sing hungry

Child of Thunder

The calling in my blood
will poison the well
a gesture frozen
in the tenuous grasp
of bitter remembrance
Must I play hide and seek
with old shadows?
Inventing a lie is second nature
for a child of thunder
dancing with scissors
to the silent drum of the moon
death is a song known by all
the lucky ones making a living out of it
the rest of us,
quote the voice of their bones

What Life Makes Me Do

Cold is the ground
and object of my rage
love lies out of sound
with fallen tears of age

Words on the wind
yellow pages soaked through
timid amalgamations
with what life makes me do

As old phases of new moons
and whiskey blues fills the jar
ghosts of heartache and I commune
until morning kidnaps my star

Please Like This

Rescue me from this insomnia
self-induced, up at odd hours
messenger of the world
bastard anchor in my hand
its copper-wired opinions
sneaking in like assassins
crawling around inside my mind
only to fight like birds on fire
pour my whiskey like the sun
and I'll chew the clouds
this calloused soul has taken the bait
spinning you tales of freedom
laced in beckoning green
moonlight and birdsong
until it's time to dance and be seen
hoping you'll bless me
with a tap on your screen

Dream-walking Siren

My dream-walking siren
of nevermore hours
wore slippers of moonlight
as she gathered her flowers

The smallest impressions
of yesterday's fairytale
false memories sweetly stitched
of this solitude I wail

Sunflower ruffles
and spotted buds abound
a final love letter carved
into marble on the ground

Beneath the frosted orchard
where fingers did entwine
a fitful slumber now will sigh
in the grave beside mine

A Different Light

Melody of dusk sets the stage
a dance with the winding dark
my memory box upended
images of you
green eyes in bottle glass glimmer
my shirt fit you like a gown
music held us like perfume
a dumb ghost I become
in these sweet desperate hours
mythology of poetry
in a diffcrent light
where moon-drawn wishes
tear verses out of me
and shadows pretend to listen

The Poet Leans Graveward

Birth predicts death
just do what you're told
so says the bone dry voice
of a god named fate
iron shoes,
strapped on for the dance
mother midnight waits up
like an unburnt eclipse
hunger's cold fire
clocks the tide
driving the mortal ghost
in what remains
the poet leans graveward
hoarding metaphors like
lost secrets underneath
the printed skirt of time

Lover of Mine

The sea ties the moon
pulling silver lightness below
and so my spindrift pages
rest in a coffin of poems
lover of mine
your torrid clown
is at your service
set us up for one more last call
pour your chaos and mine
over the rocks
and we'll weave echoes
into the white noise of the world

Same End of the Stars

Love is distorted reflections
laughing at ourselves
in street shop windows
aimless in our wandering
like the cracks in the sidewalk
love is a cliff to climb down
where I carve your name
into its cool face
and love is a night sky
drunk on galaxies
through distant eyes
if only this night could find us
on the same end of the stars

Thorn to Your Rose

Chalk up this night
to another lost cause
sleep won't come
as insomnia afflicts
with her caliginous flame
midnight worries
and this whiskey inkwell
bleed me dry
enemies to perfection
and the words in my hands
a haphazard rendering
frozen to the page
where my love
is ever a thorn to your rose
beautifully enacted
but tragically performed

Marching Heart

Last night I dreamt of drowning
tied in knots
iron mercy of floodgates
left open
lungs burning like brandy
a marching heart
wore out its welcome
my twin flame
weaving with the wild angels
sang warnings in thunder
come shine your light
into this dark folly
I've no appetite for the
wrath of the heartbroken

Beggars at the Castle

Sadness arrives at my window
I write to you in my breath on glass
spectral shades of backward darkness
mirroring twists of wide awake dreams
where ghosts claw the walls
like beggars at the castle
laughter stabbing to the bone
until pieces of me fall away
fading into the deep

Wearing the War

Stretched at the seams
by duality of this mind
once-blind eyes, failing again
and hopes pinned to the moon
mocked by voices in my head
returning, without warning
a running river
unseen, underground
unable to pick the locks
on my youth
I scrape up a dream with
my grandfather's old knife
and promise to live
like I'm told
wearing the war
as I peel with age

Hard to Love

A dream angel
ruffles her feathers
fantasy of escape
lies in secrets the poet keeps
aches I cannot name
where echoes of memory
are trees that yield no wood
and whiskey, like the rain
falls right through me to the ground
my story to tell lives on the horizon
but the weight of the sky
makes me hard to love
when bells of battered ships
on this storm clouded ocean
mirror my reality

Burden of Wolves

Merciless memories
pin me down in the corner of night
I sleep in fever
of a hand that was lent
storming inside my open door
twisting in the fury of a lover's eye
where help became hurt
coated in the dust
of a disintegrated moon
my heart and me
split the burden of wolves
as constellations burn
in traces of light
under a tipsy skyline

Photo: Eerik

Ghosts of Broken Hearts

Stray me from this sunken path
of hostile negotiations
with the hourglass
bartering time
as yesterdays rain
from the faucet of oblivion
dashed hopes are the strange remains
that swirl the drain
and ghosts of broken hearts
stand-in for God
as we dance
to nocturnal songs at 3 am
in the light of stars
that just live to die

Where Stars Make Their Bed

Black hearts boil
tears freeze in flames
such eloquent sinners
with unspoken names

Merciless greed
of imperfect shades
scattered bones,
rusted blades

Day treads the world
night's empty grave is fed
colder than the heavens
where stars make their bed

Misfortune mourned, though
by their own noose they swing
when promises of false gods
mean not a thing

Business of Words

Baleful occupation
this business of words
bells of bedlam ring
through my open door
as wraith-like memories
beat the windows
I camouflage my conscience
in vertical lines
of a hanging moon
and the music
of her velvet flirtation
drumming in time
with the pulse
that counts my blood

Coming Up Empty

Morning falls down
heavier than these hands
that refuse to write
heavier than the stones I flip
in the garden that thaws
for the lying sun
coming up empty
as the blank pages that taunt
impatient as a Spring wind
but I'm too busy
checking over my shoulder
when the snakes aren't where
they're supposed to be

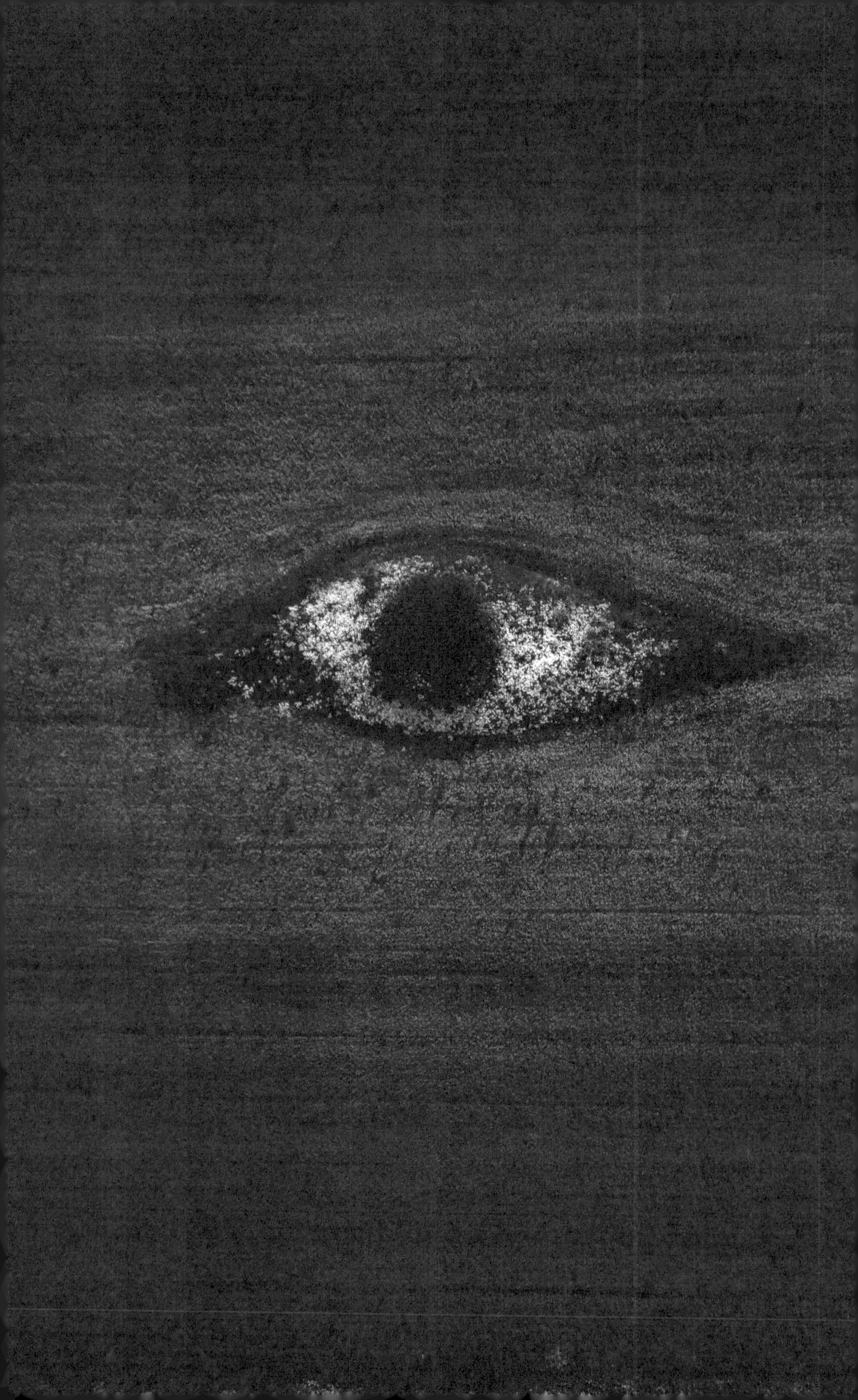

Taste of My Wishes

At the end of the beginning
damned in a trance
a dream draws its breath
as beautiful ghosts dance

Heartache of fake beauty
how cold that dish is
but in emerald eyes my poetry resides
with the splintered taste of my wishes

Photo: Egor Vikhrev

Broken Roses

Sunset is here
to undo the day
and while I can still see
the blood red smoke
of a burning glass sky
now, I wait to be swept along
in the lucid elegance
of this dark side of beautiful
fallen prey to judgement
and poetry's truth,
my ghosts and I dance
among broken roses
on the road to a perfect oblivion

Maze of Fools

Into a life of hours
we rise
angry guests
with eyes wide shut
still I paint the walls
in thin dark hues
hiding scratches
where my portrait
was ripped down
transfuse me with the sea
in a duct of lulling tides
no more to wander
a maze of fools
against a clock
that doesn't play fair

Winter's Woes

All seemed well as darkness fell
on two creatures of night
chapped lips and
hands like sparrows
in auroral bonfire light
parked cars and whiskey jars
'neath the pale head of the moon
now winter's woes are wrapped
in new words for sale
just in time
for the magnolias to bloom

Painting Fate

My war with yesterday
holds me in a chaotic embrace
I'm toeing the line
along the bluest oblivion
looking for gods
amongst the bones
and butterfly wings
painting fate
with the blood of my hands
it seems roses get restless
at the mention of heaven
instead of just dying on the vine

Broken Glass

I ride a dream to the garden
where love merges the air
a burn so wild
like the fire in your hair

You sing to me of flowers,
moonlight on grass
midnight serenades
in our language of broken glass

A fantasy of escape
from empty halls of shame
where whiskey stains my laughter
and regret knows my name

My Own Dark

The wind is not shy
as it speaks to the trees
there being no way
to know what is said
in its beautiful undoing
so go on and question
how loudly I speak to the moon
means nothing to me
poetic lines, I find
in every drop of her shine
dancing in my own dark
while shadows tend the fire

Chapters Within You

I am but a fool
to the sad eyes
that hold me
I face the bleeding edge
where bones dream
no courage to speak
but I move my lips
in poetic limerence
as the moon is replaced
by the luminous clock
cracked along
my threadbare spine
like the volumes
of chapters within you
where I walk so heavily
and each graceful swoop
becomes a jumbled toss

Photo: Annie Spratt

Comets in my Blood

Night begins
its somber introduction
cerulean whispers topple
within a crepuscular motion
until an alabaster moon
ignites comets in my blood
an auroral haze of green
and its promise of peace
falls on the dark forest
where I'm bound
carving myself
from what remains
aching for the kiss
that eludes me so

Undertaker's Graffiti

Tangled in tangents
of a retreating world
lassitude knows no bounds
walking dead with heads in the sand
choke on dust's grainy texture
how I long to escape
gummy pavements
that kill my vibe
hide me from pandemonium
being no poet of chaos culture
I find lost lyrics
in shadows of the wind,
whiskey and moonlight
being my only friends
bleached bones
and secrets left behind
become undertaker's graffiti

My Opus, Untitled

Rip these doors from their hinges
and mend the rain with your hair
walk me not to degradation
on this journey home
I drag my feet
upon the burning tightrope
as my muse dances her ring of fire
I'll use my own bones
for crutches when I fall
my opus, untitled
on pages once lost in a book
are now torn to the wild

Returned to Sender

Amidst the ashen vacancy
of the street's bones
I loll with deaf indifference
voices murmur like water
slaving for an emptiness
that could swallow the dark
my quill long dulled
drips my whiskey blood
as poetry falls on deaf ears
these letters to humanity
are always returned to sender
shame is bound to dance
along the rim of the wishing well
so I'll cloak this sadness
in a stolen voice
and wait right here
until the moon
lights me on fire

Raindrop in the Sun

My thoughts hitch a ride
on a ghost white cloud
ballooning lyrics from
the tongue of a poet
pebbles to a crow
I scrounge them all
finger painting mirages
beyond my window
dyeing my days horizontal
burning with thirst
like a raindrop in the sun

Silent Traveler

Sing of home
for this silent traveler
stomp the boards
to my whispers
wishing time backwards
across neptunian furrows
to our vacant days
I melt in the heat
of gunshot eyes
and hope
is but a fly on the wall
watching me tie moonbeams
around my heart
bound and waiting
just to feel her reflection

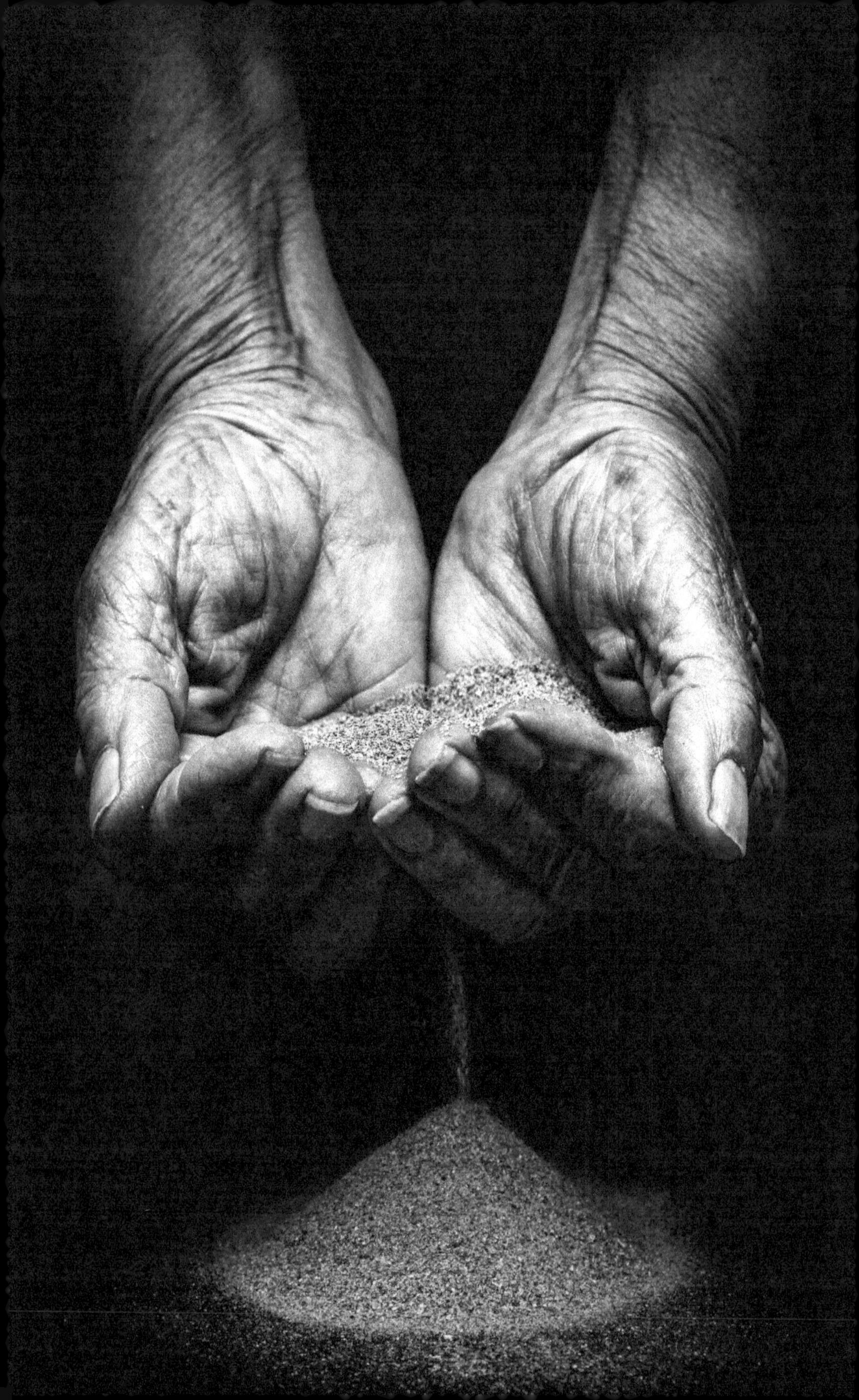

Silent Parade

Boxed in by the hourglass
time does not hold still
decomposing the past
as secrets tie a tongue
infused with indecision
another marcher
in a silent parade
of the night's bitter broken
I echo the voices
in mirroring moonlight
and paint them shouting
bleeding me of reason
as dreams flow
like rainwater from my pen
maybe then
someone will hear me

Photo: ojos de hojalata

Ghosts of a Love

Long after the sun
unearths our bones
the meadow whispers
its waking tones

Rustling shade,
robins on the wing
draped in blue
how hearts did sing

Upon this charred ground
where the moon loaned her spark
now dance ghosts of a love
written in the dark

Imposter Tongue

I seek out words to excite oblivion
tumbling through hollows
where doves take shelter
my imposter tongue
painting secrets in smoldering ink
to become beautiful lies
or maybe, just maybe, labyrinthine truths
exhausted hope delays the inevitable
spilling as indifference on the page
still I juggle knives with closed eyes
and wait for the blades to pass through
my god-in-the-moon is nothing more
than a kite with no string

Moonblind Ghost

I tap dance on ticking time-bombs
at the edge of wasted years
dreams bleed out, capsized in chains
rusted bonds to hold me here

Fragmented poetry of forgotten names
my lungs burn in hostile air
when a moonblind ghost begs the sky to fall
self sabotage has come to bear

Wars of Words

The first strip of sunlight
torn from stubborn sky
a darksome undertow
becomes ripples in the tide

Prayers of water music
clamor with lost dreams
this cloak of the poet
keeps tearing at the seams

Dawn paints the cliff
and its whispering stones
in whitewashed tragedy
of my ancestors' bones

Wars of words twist my tongue
so I'll never quell this hunger
especially when a thousand fears
volley back in thunder

The pen in my hand held like a grudge
with no verse left to chance
accepting my fate that with this fire
I was born to dance

Made for Now

We ride the world like a carousel
a cosmic wheel of chance
waiting for heaven to crack open
spilling hidden secrets
between moon clouds
Who will warn the stars
before they burn?
Sifting truth from fiction
within man made borders
strip me down to my flaws
to hear the voice of my bones
and how it sings for you
poetry is an homage
to my wandering worry
where tomorrow scares me to death
so let's revel in today's sun
until we find god in the rain
sipping breaths of the shoreline
and its sea breeze sighs
this is how we were made to love
we were made for now

Missed the Memo

Hung by the toes
from a trapeze with no net
in the fury and weight of morning
clinging to my last breath of the night
until the blood clots in my fingers
I cage my dreams
and paint them in whispers
for you, my vacant girl with firefly eyes
follow the smoke
and sift me from the rubble
when you get here
but for now I can't think
with my ears so full of birdsong
I guess they missed the memo

Through Nowhere Eyes

I look for someday
through nowhere eyes
slipping on footprints
as rhymes go dormant
awaiting karma's kiss
dancing in the haze
at every dead end in the maze
while the current of memories
molds my heart
and breaks me a little more
with each forgotten song

Heavy are my Hands

Heavy are my hands
in this trepidation overdrive
counting off catastrophes
on my fingers one by one
helpless I've become
to stifle the cries
of the dark horse
wild and untethered
losing my own name
on the way home
bleeding like the sky
behind a crying sunset
wondering what it was
the clouds had to say

Blue is my Muse

I wait for spring
to thaw this winter blood
fractured behind
a not-so-holy countenance
weight of the world
does not help me breathe
blue is my muse
when love is your name
thumbing petals
of your wicked wild
in the saffron canyon
of my heart's twilight illusion
behind this mask
a ghost writer in hiding burns
awaiting poetry's butterfly effect
immersed in the art
I break myself to create

Rain Falls Through Me

Incarcerated
with mutiny in my bones
the ghost with a frostbite smile
lifts its boot off my chest
love never given
has honeyed my blood
I'm still on my back
as pain steals off
and rain falls through me
I drink of the waters
that flood the night
cleansing my tongue
of the ash from so many fires ago

Wreckage of My Dreams

Vibrations of the moon
entwine mounting screams
silver sounds of light
in wreckage of my dreams

Wet wings are wrung
from rain's halfway winds
the clock's engine toils
for hands that blindly spin

A poetry of passion
and wounds bitterly mended
now lies amongst the rubble
of walls so poorly defended

Photo: Patrick Schöpflin

My Half of the Sky

A forbidden dance
in the lowest of light
our velveteen forest
feeling the pull of midnight

Hypnotized in the serenade
of your endless name
with each wild breath
drawn from the flame

'Neath tendrils of stardust
oh how the heavens weep
for my half of the sky,
like this reckless love,
is yours to keep

Nowhere to Run

I'd set fire to this unkind world
just to gather ashes in silence
a shipwrecked heart
mirroring voices
that paint beautiful lies
by the numbers
with loaded guns I sit
with nowhere to run
on another lonely night
that wasn't worth the whiskey

Petals Against a Boulder

My wild tongue knows not
the wisdom of age
too many hands adorn the clock
on my moon colored walls
where darkness is used up
keys to the kingdom rust away
as hell's wind stirs the sea
with pious voices of living dead
words flutter
just petals against a boulder
so, like the sky
I remain indifferent

Delicate Asylum

I have bled out
for this narrative
punished by a past
bound in lovely bones
and hating eyes
history, as it's told
becomes fertilizer
for a garden of secrets
this monotone poetry its only crop
free me from these shackles
of my own making
take me into your delicate asylum
I'll burn under your handprints
beneath the shadows
of the backwoods
where our cries wake the ghosts
that push the moon around

Sacred Ground

Folding from the weight of what I've become
shouldering the cloak
of loneliness as the shore wears the ocean
tonight the stars sing an unfamiliar song
threading scars across a charcoal sky
like a reckless heart
never breaking apart the same way twice
though devoured dreams
inhabit the pockets of my soul
I hold your place on this sacred ground
where I rode the lightning of your kiss
as atomic strands painted your face
and your eyes spoke a million poems

Wasted Time

Help me sacrifice this fury
a little dance in drunk repose
grease on the squeaky wheel
that keeps me awake at night
where old songs burn
with the question of home
in dreams I cannot measure
and ghosts are as bold as the love
that splinters and cracks
along the edge of wasted time

Somewhere in the Night

Lured to the brink by confessions
to appease absent gods
ghosts of my wounds
burn my bones
electrical shading
in storms of caged ink
where my words
decorate the pages
and all but drown
in the chaotic chant of the sea
like wandering crows
lost somewhere in the night
with no map to the horizon

Paper Doll

Hesitant is my appetite
for reality's sharp sting
cradle in sideways dreams of skylight
this paper doll on a string

Reasoning with destiny
in poetry of lucky love
and stale ghosts of childhood phase
wrapping riddles around each night to come
and all those yesterdays

A Statue I've Become

I wear my mistakes
in scars on my chest
you can connect the dots if you wish
my diatribe of falling echoes
drones on with the
hoarse hum of the wind
a statue I've become
in time's garden that never blooms
molded in the clay of a distant shore
along the same river that flows in your name
and wets your ankles as you dance
from stone to stone
butterflies aflame laugh at my predicament
If only the moon
would pretend to give a damn

Photo: DuxX

A Tale to Savor

Night sky teases a tale to savor
northern lights dance
like shadows of wild horses
I sing of your eyes
those green gods
my brown voice
your pursed lips
wearing my dreams
ribboned around your waist
heat undoes itself
in a mane of smoke
and midnight dust
held to the ground
where earth sounds like poetry
until we wake
beside the morning
and dandelions conspire
to spread the word

Broken As My Sleep

In the middle of silence
seclusion's ghost I bear
through circles of light we dance
as if you are still there

Talking to walls,
picking the locks
as your footsteps breeze
through my memory box

A poverty of skin
where I countenance to weep
then lay it out in verses
as broken as my sleep

Lonely in my Veins

This beautiful lonely in my veins
redder than the roses
that bloom in your name
tonight the moon calls me
to the meadow where love raged
and the whippoorwill is moaning
his melancholy blues
oh this beautiful lonely in my veins

Photo: Bisli

Acknowledgements

I could say Thank You a million times and still not begin to convey my appreciation to all my family and friends that have been there from day one and continue to support me in this endeavor. You guys rock and I love you all!

Most importantly, to my sweetheart Rae, your love and support mean the absolute world to me. You faithfully wear the hats of a confidant, muse, and (unpaid) editor. I could never have done this without you.

Much love to all,
DSP

JR Hataway (Dead Society Poet) spends most of his time as a towboat captain on the inland rivers of the United States. He found a love for poetry and prose after discovering the works of Jim Harrison, Charles Bukowski, and Dylan Thomas along with many others. When not on the water you will find him somewhere along the backroads of Alabama with his dog, Petey.

JR Hataway

Also Available

- A Walk After Midnight: Musings by Dead Society Poet
- Lend Me Your Fire: Poems of love and longing by Dead Society Poet
- Homesick Angels & Second-hand Roses: Reflections of a Dead Society Poet
- Bar Napkin Love Letters: Blurred lines from Dead Society Poet

Available from all major booksellers!

Reviews

Praise for Dead Society Poet:

"These beautiful writes deserve our attention."
(Amazon review/Lend Me Your Fire)

"If you're looking for a collection that tugs at your soul, "Bar Napkin
Love Letters" is it."
(Amazon review)

"…deliciously decadent. A Must Read!"
(Amazon review/Homesick Angels & Second-hand Roses)

"Beautifully written and boldly spoken poetry. Loved it!!"
(Amazon review/A Walk After Midnight)